Mennonite Life

JOHN A. HOSTETLER

Mennonite Life

JOHN A. HOSTETLER

Herald Press

SCOTTDALE, PENNSYLVANIA/KITCHENER, ONTARIO

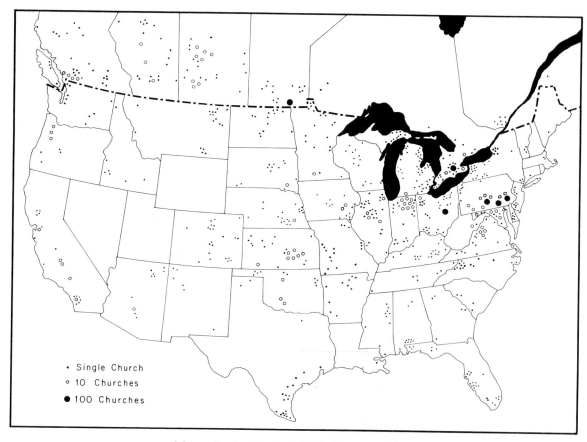

Mennonite churches in the United States and Canada.

MENNONITE LIFE, copyright © 1983 by Herald Press, Scottdale, Pa. 15683
Published simultaneously in Canada by Herald Press, Kitchener, Ont. N2G 4M5
Library of Congress Catalog Card Number: 82-83962
International Standard Book Number: 0-8361-1995-9
Printed in the United States of America
Design by Sue Bishop
83 84 85 86 87 10 9 8 7 6 5 4 3 2 1

The Mennonite Obscurity

The Mennonites came to America a century before the country was founded and today their members live in all parts of the United States and in every province of Canada. They are one of the best documented religious minorities in America. But despite their long history and their conspicuous presence, they are often falsely identified with related groups like their colorful cousins, the Amish, or linked with exotic religious practices such as shunning.

There are reasons for confusion. The Mennonites are only one of several so-called Pennsylvania Dutch groups that settled in William Penn's colony in America. Other Germanic groups who settled there included the Moravians, Schwenkfelders, and German Baptist Brethren. From their beginning in the sixteenth-century Mennonites took exception to state religion and established their own churches. They acquired many uncomplimentary nicknames along the way. Because the Mennonites themselves are of diverse cultural origin—Swiss, German, and Dutch—and because local communities differ in the details of religious life and custom, the confusion is compounded.

Thus not all Mennonites look alike, sing the same songs, have German-sounding names, nor talk about their faith in the same way. In fact, Mennonites of various races now live in forty nations and speak many languages. However, this book highlights the North American Mennonites with limited reference to their life and activity in other places.

Plain and Fancy

The wide variety in dress and customs among different Mennonite groups—some plain and some nonplain—is a major source of confusion to the tourist. Many associate plain garb with Mennonites and erroneously conclude that nonplain people cannot be Mennonite. That

Mennonites are made up of both "plain" and "fancy" subgroups is for most outsiders not comprehended.

The terms "plain" and "fancy" have long been used among the Pennsylvania German-speaking groups. "Plain" refers to distinctive dress and grooming patterns. Those who did not wear distinctive dress, or those who rejected the discipline of their group were called "fancy." They were "fancy" because their dress no longer identified them as simple or humble people.

Today most Mennonite groups can be arranged on a scale from the very traditional to various degrees of modernity. Like other religious traditions, Jewish or Protestant, Mennonite social practices include a wide spectrum. In Mennonite circles the traditional groups retain more familistic elements of life than those groups who have accommodated to individualistic pursuits and city life.

The Mennonite ideal is a spiritual community of persons who have individually and collectively committed their loyalties to God and to each other, and who attempt to practice the ethics of Jesus within a specific community. Their understanding of the gospel emphasizes reconciliation and peace. Maintaining a community, caring and sharing, and consistency of life are important to the Mennonite people. The character and consistency of these practices, of course, varies. Community is for them not only a human support system but a redemptive process. Living as a corporate body in trusting relationships is seen as a love-response to God. The consequences of conversion, for Mennonites, means participation in a believing community, a way of life, having the qualities of quiet composure, peace, and willingness to suffer for the faith.

Origin

The Mennonites are spiritual descendants of the Anabaptists of sixteenth-century Europe, a renewal movement emphasizing faithful discipleship to the teachings of Jesus and separation of church and

Menno Simons, teacher and expositor of Anabaptism in the Netherlands
and North Germany.

state. The term Anabaptist, meaning twice-baptized, was a nickname they acquired from those who considered them a dangerous influence. The movement objected to the baptism of babies, believing that infants have no knowledge of sin, and that baptism was intended for believing adults. Freedom of conscience, freedom of religious association, and personal responsibility for making decisions was important to them.

The Anabaptists objected to a state church that forced everyone to be a member, while keeping the masses spirituality illiterate. They rejected the idea that ritual ceremonies could transfuse the grace of God into the soul of a person. The city council of Zurich resisted the Anabaptist reforms, and a small circle of believers began to meet secretly in homes. On the evening of January 21, 1525, in a moment of inspiration, a group of persons baptized each other, against the rule of the civil authorities. They did so, knowing that they would face "tyranny, torture, sword, fire, or water." A prominent founder of Swiss Anabaptism was Conrad Grebel of Zurich.

The house-church movement spread among the common people to other German-speaking areas, and to the Netherlands. Ten years after the break in Zurich, a priest in the Netherlands by the name of Menno Simons began doubting the Catholic doctrine of the mass. Did the bread which he held in his hands literally turn into the flesh of Jesus every time he conducted mass? Menno soon had second thoughts about infant baptism also, and he began searching the Bible.

Menno Simons joined the Anabaptist movement in 1536 and became an ardent organizer of underground house-church groups. He preached, admonished, debated, and wrote long explanations of the new reforms for the rest of his life. The learned doctors of the state church, he said, were blinded to the simplicity of the teachings of the Bible. The common people were, in his words, nourished on "legends, fables, holy days, images, holy water, confessionals, pilgrimages, vespers, and offerings." Menno Simons was a dynamic teacher and organizer of Anabaptism in the Netherlands and his followers became known as Mennonites.

"Plain" Mennonite schoolchildren.

Distinctive Beliefs

The early Anabaptist-Mennonites rejected formalized ceremonies (like the mass) and insisted on "following Christ in life"—or a change of character followed by Christian conduct. To the authorities, such claims seemed presumptuous and arrogant. Not only the medieval church, but the newly formed Lutheran and Reformed territorial churches felt threatened by the Anabaptist movement. As the only authorized churches in their territory, they suppressed and banished the Anabaptists as outlaws, arguing that unless infants were baptized and religious ceremonies were conducted by the state approved church, society would become pagan and collapse.

Laws were enacted to prevent persons from taking up Anabaptist beliefs. But in spite of this, the movement grew rapidly. The large Anabaptist-Mennonite martyr book called *Martyrs Mirror* (Herald Press), contains accounts of more than 4,000 burnings of individuals, numerous stonings, crucifixions, imprisonments, brandings, burials alive, suffocations, severing of limbs, and other atrocities.

The Anabaptists were confronted not only with the strong ecclesiastical order, but with fanatical fringe groups among their sympathizers. Some of these zealous individuals plundered churches, advocated violence, and were intolerant of persons who would not aid in social reforms; others depended on dreams and revelations to support their extreme behavior. Notwithstanding, the Mennonites emerged as the "peaceful" Anabaptists who advocated love and nonresistance. Deploring the tragic events of violent revolution, Menno Simons taught his followers that prophecy, visions, and reason had to be checked against the Bible and understood from the examples of the life of Jesus.

During the Reformation period Mennonite beliefs differed from those of Martin Luther and John Calvin in two respects: (1) in the meaning of being Christian, and (2) in the definition of church. The Mennonites reasoned that being Christian meant "following Christ in life." This included generously sharing with those in need, practicing love and Christian nonresistance, and maintaining a Christian brother-

Mennonite students of music at a retreat center.

Mennonite worship assembly. Salford congregation.

Early Pennsylvania Mennonite meetinghouse
still in use. Methacton congregation.

hood. While Luther and Calvin stressed "the preaching of the Word," the Anabaptist-Mennonites emphasized the necessity of living in a "love community" separate from the war-waging and political functions of society.

The established churches of the Reformation period could think of Jesus as a dying savior, a future judge, but not as an example to follow in life. That would have been considered arrogant. It was reasoned that even the best of the clergy could not do that! The Mennonites to this day insist on practicing what other Christians frequently call "the hard sayings" of Jesus—avoiding courts to settle disputes, not swearing or taking an oath, and not resisting one's enemies. Because of their intent to do good, practice honesty, patience, and uprightness, Mennonites have often been called "works-saints," "heaven-stormers," or similar nicknames by those who have little sympathy for their beliefs.

The church is for Mennonites a voluntary brotherhood, a believing communion where "the rule of Christ" is practiced. As such, this body is made up of believers who reconcile their relationships with each other in spite of their differences. The Mennonite people meet each Sunday in church buildings or meetinghouses for singing, prayer, worship, sharing, Bible study, and fellowship. Their ceremonies include water baptism and the Lord's supper. Among some, foot washing (as a symbol of humility and brotherhood) is also observed in conjunction with the Lord's supper.

Tender Conscience

An important guideline for living, Mennonites hold, is contained in the words of Jesus, "You have heard that it was said, 'You shall love your neighbor and hate your enemy.' But I say to you, Love your enemies and pray for those who persecute you" (Matthew 5:43–44). Although it is human to have enemies, the Mennonite people hold that Christians must return good for evil, whether the enemy is personal or collective. About 12,000 Mennonite young men refused military service

Old Order Mennonite meeting and cemetery.
Conestoga congregation, Ontario.

in the United States during World War II. Instead they worked in mental hospitals and in soil conservation service, all of it financed by the church.

The reason for loving the enemy lies not in achieving political ends, but in loving obedience to the teaching of Jesus. The practice of returning good for evil requires spiritual qualities not apparent to the human way of thinking. Mennonites believe that true Christians are called and set aside for a profound spiritual struggle, however difficult and humiliating. The practice of nonresistance involves readiness to suffer injustice in a spirit of meekness, and the refusal to use violence and bloodshed in human relations.

Throughout history the Mennonites have been a small minority within the Christian tradition. Indeed, Mennonites have often been labeled as traitors or parties to leftist or rightist movements. While their commitment to nonviolence as a way of life may seem radical to some, to them it suggests a deeper resource, a spiritual witness against wrong uses of power, status, and wealth. Practices which would implicate them in the use of coercion and in the "evil" structures of society are avoided on principle.

Today the Mennonite attitude toward government is essentially like that of their early founders. To overthrow a government would be considered unchristian. However, civil disobedience may sometimes become necessary. Like the early founders, the Mennonites place a major limitation on the authority of the state. The state has no jurisdiction over the spiritual realm, they believe, no right to promote religious uniformity nor to suppress dissent. The state may not assume the functions of conscience, take over the individual's responsibility to God, nor educate the children against the wishes of the parents.

Stewards of the Soil

Because of religious persecution and intolerance the Mennonites have migrated often in their history. Many of the German-speaking groups who left their European homelands came to North America, founding their first surviving community in Pennsylvania as early as 1683. Their descendants are living largely in the western part of the United States. The Mennonites of the Netherlands and North Germany migrated to the Vistula Delta (now Poland), later to South Russia, and finally to the Great Plains of the United States and Canada in several different periods, especially from 1873 to 1874, 1922 to 1930, and from 1943 to 1948. During the latter two periods many located in Mexico, Brazil, and Paraguay. Many Mennonites, however, remained in Europe.

The Mennonites have excelled as farmers in all countries where they have settled. The prevailing intolerance for their religion drove them to submarginal, mountainous, and swamplands, where they exercised diligence, thrift, and creativity. In the Emmental Valley and the Jura Mountains of Switzerland they developed new breeds of dairy cattle and horses, new varieties of clover crops, made fine cheeses, and wove good quality linens.

In Germany Mennonites developed new farming practices and were cited as master farmers by agricultural associations and by government departments. On the opposite side of the Rhine in France it was the same. The orderly farm fields and the improved economic standing of the Mennonite farms stood in sharp contrast to those of the native populations. Their success gave rise to a popular belief that the Mennonites were endowed with supernatural farming secrets.

In Poland where the Dutch Mennonites settled as refugees, they transformed swamps and lowlands into highly productive territory. On a forty-mile front, they managed to drain lands that lay below sea level. They constructed windmills and cleared the land of brush and undergrowth. Permanently protecting the productive fields against the danger of the rising Baltic waters, the rainy seasons, the north winds, and the snow thaws, was a gigantic undertaking requiring communal effort and a sense of the common good. In addition to grain production, they maintained high quality dairy herds and developed the arts of gardening and cheese-making.

Witmarsum Mennonite Church, Brazil.

Emmental Mennonite meetinghouse, Langnau, Switzerland.

Entrance to the Singel Mennonite Church,
Amsterdam, Netherlands.

Mennonites in eastern Pennsylvania.

When the Dutch-Polish Mennonites migrated to South Russia at the end of the eighteenth century they settled on vast arid lands. In a few generations they transformed the barren steppes (or plains) from a pasture and sheep grazing region into "the granary of Europe." They successfully introduced fruit, shade, and mulberry trees. In twenty years they planted over five million trees in hundreds of villages. Mennonite agricultural experts developed new breeds of cattle as well as road and draft horses. The so-called Soviet or Red Cow, widespread today in Russia, derives from a breed of dairy cattle developed years ago by the Mennonites.

While living on the plains of South Russia, the Mennonites tried to develop new varieties of grain adapted to that climate. The steppes consisted of a vast stretch of level grassy land with few trees, with extremely cold weather in winter and scorching heat in the summer. Mennonite agriculturalists produced a special type of grain called Turkey Hard Winter wheat. Flour made from it was not only more nutritious, but the wheat yielded better with less rainfall, and it had greater resistance to plant disease than did other known varieties. Turkey Hard Winter wheat found its way to Kansas with the Mennonite immigration, and today this wheat is recognized as the grandfather variety of all types of hard winter wheat grown in the United States.

The Mennonites in Russia also devised new farm implements suited for the great plains they were farming. They made multiple-share plows, harrows, wagons, cutters, seed-cleaning mills, threshing machines, and various types of engines. Several large factories and many smaller ones produced one tenth of the total Russian output of farm equipment. With the advent of the communist revolution the Mennonite settlements were dissolved and South Russia lost its most productive farmers. Those who resettled in Paraguay, Canada, and the United States continue to practice their agricultural skills.

The agricultural contributions of the Mennonites to America have been widely recognized. In the United States most immigrant Mennonite families located on individualized farms rather than villages. Some of the agricultural counties with the highest per capita farm income are heavily populated with Mennonite farms.

Rural living, backed by a solid agricultural economy, has for centuries been considered the norm among some Mennonites. This belief has at times been so strong among some groups that persons were required to farm in order to be church members. Living in isolation, especially in colonies and villages, guaranteed separation and protection from "the world." But such isolation frequently resulted in strong group-centered attitudes whereby members came to think of themselves as a special people, with a distinct language and dress code.

City Mennonites

Urbanization in the twentieth century has introduced unprecedented changes among American Mennonites. The young began to attend schools of higher education in large numbers, and Mennonites established their own secondary schools and colleges. Presently not more than 20 percent of American Mennonite households are engaged in farming. Some churches have more members living in the city than in the country or in small towns. There are Mennonite churches in large cities, including Toronto, Winnipeg, Los Angeles, Chicago, Philadelphia, New York, and Phoenix. The membership in city churches consists of many diverse cultural groups.

The tension between traditional values and modern trends in the American environment has resulted in various forms of accommodation and response. Some have rejected the faith and all pretensions of being Mennonite. In large urban centers like New York, Philadelphia, and Denver, for example, there are scores of former Mennonites who do not identify with the church. Others have become marginal Mennonites, retaining a nostalgic interest in the tradition. Still others have attempted to relate their heritage in a meaningful way to the social issues and opportunities of the twentieth century. Many young Mennonites are showing a renewed interest in their historical roots.

Conservative Mennonite children with black straw hats.

Among progressive Mennonites dress patterns have changed,
but many social customs are passed on.

The "Plain" Mennonites

Both Swiss and Dutch streams of Mennonitism have traditional subgroups designated by the prefix "Old" or "Old Order." Among those of Swiss origin are the Old Order Mennonites and the Old Order Amish Mennonites. Both groups maintain farming communities and are distinguished by their horse-and-buggy culture and by their "plain" garb. The Old Order Mennonites reside in Pennsylvania, Virginia, Ohio, Indiana, Missouri, and Ontario. They assemble for worship in simple meetinghouses. Divisions among the Old Order Mennonites have given rise to such special subgroups as the "Black Bumper" Mennonites who are allowed automobiles, if everything, including the chrome, is painted black.

The Amish derive from Jacob Ammann, a leader among the Swiss and Alsatian Mennonites, who emphasized a return to orthodoxy. The Amish are widely recognized today for their distinctive way of life, their farming practices, and for resisting trends toward large-scale technology, higher education, and compulsory welfare programs. The Amish people live on family farms around small rural towns and are neighbors to non-Amish households. They assemble in their farm homes for worship and speak a dialect (derived from Upper Rhineland Germany) called Pennsylvania German. They install neither electricity nor telephones in their homes. Their communities are concentrated in Pennsylvania, Ohio, and Indiana, though there are Amish communities in twenty states.

The "plain" element among the Dutch Mennonites is preserved in the Old Colony Mennonites who migrated by way of Prussia (now Poland) and Russia to Canada and later moved to Mexico and other South American countries. The Old Colonists have preserved the village settlement pattern in full as it was in Russia. Large acreages are purchased by Mennonite village corporations and then resold to family units in the village. Each village is governed by a council that oversees both economic and religious aspects of life. Old Colony villages are striking examples of cultural and religious islands, severely limiting interaction with the surrounding populations. The Old Colony Mennonites speak a low-German dialect (*Platt-deutsch*), very different from the Rhineland (Pennsylvania German) dialect of the Amish. Both groups resist the trend toward modernization and affluent living.

A Caring and Sharing People

Many branches of the Mennonites work cooperatively through the Mennonite Central Committee (MCC) in a worldwide service to aid suffering and deprived peoples. Organized in 1920 during the Bolshevik Revolution in Russia to help famine-stricken people, this organization continues to respond to victims of famine or disaster in places like Southeast Asia, Africa, the Middle East, and in North America.

Liberating people from famine, poverty, disease, illiteracy, and malnutrition takes many forms. During periods of suffering or disaster the Mennonites send food and garments, distributed by their own people, to needy places. A portable steam canner processes food in various Mennonite regions. Whole communities respond by donating food which is shipped abroad. Men and women work long days over hot stoves, from spring to fall, according to need.

Garment collection centers operate in strategic locations from California to Pennsylvania and from Vancouver to Ottawa. The garments are carefully examined, cleaned, mended, baled, and labeled for shipment. Each year gifts of soap, towels, and clothing are prepared for overseas shipment. Materials go to the needy regardless of race or religion. As much as possible, Mennonite workers accompany the food and clothing for distribution. Cash donations are raised primarily through offerings in churches and augmented by auction sales and thrift stores in Mennonite communities.

The MCC organization has grown in scope to involve agriculturalists, engineers, and others skilled in intermediate technology and

French Mennonite house-barn in Alsace.

Swiss bank-barn architecture in Pennsylvania.

Character studies of Russian Mennonites. Abraham Dyck and Elizabeth Epp symbolize a sturdy people who fell victim to revolution and starvation.

economics as needed to aid the people in liberating themselves from poverty. Nurses, doctors, and nutritionists work with native cultures in the prevention of disease and malnutrition. Teachers who volunteer for overseas service are trained and sent to Third World countries to teach in their schools. Where there are social and institutional injustices in the United States, trained workers are sent to aid miniority groups in rural and urban regions. In such ways Mennonites, as well as other Christian volunteers who accept the Mennonite understanding of the gospel of peace, help to translate into flesh and blood the command of Jesus to "love your neighbor as yourself."

Following major periods of war or famine the Mennonites have helped many refugees to find new homes. Following World War II thousands of Mennonites from Russia and Eastern Europe found new homes in Paraguay and other parts of South America. Helping these uprooted peoples to find land, tools, and technical skills has drawn the world Mennonite brotherhood closer together.

The Mennonite organization helps where the need is greatest and where it can be determined that the assistance will reach those who are in greatest need, often in areas overlooked by the news media and by other agencies. Mennonite resources are small in comparison to world need. Yet their task, as they perceive it, is to feed the hungry, clothe the naked, shelter the homeless, and bring compassion. "Our Christian call," according to a Mennonite spokesman, "is not only to send help, but to be present with those who suffer. Our people are agents of hope in the many places we work."

The MCC symbol, a dove fused with a cross and set in a globe, is a visualization of its purpose—to serve "in the name of Christ." Today MCC has over 800 persons on location in 40 countries, though the total program of aid includes 65 countries. The headquarters of the Mennonite Central Committee (MCC) in the United States is located in the small town of Akron, Pennsylvania. The Mennonites in Canada work together in a partner organization, MCC Canada, with offices in Winnipeg. The United States staff, numbering about 75 persons from all over North America, administers the worldwide ministry of service.

Incoming volunteers spend several days or weeks at Akron receiving orientation before going into service. A visitor coming to headquarters at any time may find a few of the incoming and outgoing volunteers.

Membership and Geography

The world membership of Mennonites is about 690,000 with less than half that number in North America. In the United States there are about 235,000 members and in Canada an estimated 92,000. There are Mennonite communities or churches in over forty countries outside the United States and Canada. About one third of all Mennonite members are descendants of the ethnic Mennonite heritage. Many of the newly formed churches are made up of people in Third World countries who have accepted the Mennonite faith.

The diffusion of the Mennonites from a small subculture to diverse communities in many parts of the world is an impressive but complex development. Initially, and at various times in their history, they suffered intolerance so that they migrated to other lands. Migration and colonization accounts for some of the proliferation, but so does missionary work in many countries. Although Mennonites do not generally take strong measures to recruit new members, they take seriously the command of Jesus to "go and teach all nations." Their missionary vision was aptly expressed by their leader, Menno Simons, in 1539: "True evangelical faith cannot lie dormant. It feeds the hungry, it clothes the naked, it comforts the sorrowful, it shelters the destitute, it serves those that harm it, it binds up that which is wounded, it has become all things to all men."

Most of the Mennonite communities in Europe today are located in Germany, the Netherlands, France, Switzerland. An unknown number live in Russia. These groups are descendants of the sixteenth-century founders, of persons who remained in Europe after others had migrated to the New World. The Mennonites in the Netherlands are a

Old Colony Mennonite children in Mexico.

Village of Reinland, Manitoba. This settlement pattern of
transplanted European Mennonite communities is maintained
by Old Colony Mennonites in Mexico.

small but influential Protestant denomination in that country. There are probably 95,000 members in European countries (including as many as 50,000 in Russia).

In Central and South America transplanted European Mennonite communities have taken root in Mexico, Brazil, Belize, Bolivia, Honduras, Paraguay, and Uruguay. In other Latin American countries Spanish-speaking Mennonite churches are located in Argentina, Colombia, Panama, Puerto Rico, and Jamaica. An estimated 67,000 Mennonites live in Central and South America.

In Asia there are Mennonite churches in India, Indonesia, Japan, the Philippines, Taiwan, and Vietnam. At one time there were 5,000 members in China. The first Mennonite church in Indonesia was founded by the Dutch Mennonites in 1854. The churches in India were established in the late nineteenth century following the North American Mennonite response to the physical and spiritual needs of that country. There is one church in Australia. Membership in Asia is estimated at 102,000.

The most rapid growth of Mennonites presently is occurring in Africa and Asia. The Mennonite interpretation of the gospel as reconciliation and peace has appealed greatly to some of the people in Africa. Newly formed churches in Africa are located in Ethiopia, Ghana, Kenya, Nigeria, Somalia, Tanzania, Zaire, Zambia, and Zimbabwe. The Mennonite membership in all of Africa is estimated at 98,000.

Mennonite membership circles the globe. Their communities and churches belong to many nations and races. Despite the many cultural, linguistic, and social variations, they work toward a common vision through the numerous social networks maintained among them.

Regional Centers of Mennonitism

Although the Mennonites in North America are widely disbursed, they are heavily concentrated in certain areas. After the original

Many Mennonite churches conduct summer Bible schools
in their communities.

settlement in Pennsylvania, many located on farmlands north of Philadelphia and along the Pequea and Conestoga creeks in Lancaster County. Today they are strongly represented in areas surrounding Lancaster, Souderton, Perkasie, and Doylestown. Southeastern Pennsylvania embodies the largest and oldest concentration of Mennonites in North America. Lancaster County has several of the larger Mennonite church groups as well as a diversity of smaller divisions. It also has various types of Amish, the Reformed Mennonites, the Old Order Mennonites, those who drive horse and carriage and those who use automobiles, and several smaller groups with colorful names like "Pikers" and "The 35-ers." Other Anabaptist-related groups—the Church of the Brethren (earlier called Tunkers), the River Brethren, and the Brethren in Christ—are also represented in the county. Due to its outstanding agricultural production, beautiful landscape and rolling valleys, neatly kept farm buildings and fields, Lancaster County enjoys a reputation as the "garden spot" of the world.

The Shenandoah Valley of Virginia was settled by the Mennonites as early as 1727. Although their churches and farms are scattered all along the western side of the Skyline Drive, Harrisonburg is the center of their business and professional life. Eastern Mennonite College is located in its northwest suburb of Park View. Old Order or horse and carriage Mennonites also live in the Shenandoah Valley.

A hundred miles from Niagara Falls, in southern Ontario is another distinctive Mennonite area. Surrounding the twin cities of Kitchener-Waterloo is a rich agricultural region famous for its farmers' markets, cider presses, apple butter, and jam factories. Although the Old Order groups are farmers, many of the Mennonites are professional people, merchants, and craftsmen in nearby villages such as St. Jacobs, New Dundee, and Elmira. Like the Pennsylvania settlement, it is an old community founded in 1800 by Pennsylvania Mennonites of Swiss descent, and today has probably as many branches of Mennonites as does Lancaster County. In addition there are several Mennonite groups of Dutch-Prussian-Ukranian descent in this region. Conrad

Mennonite family in India. This couple directs
a school of nursing at Dhamtari.

A Mennonite agricultural development project in rural Brazil.

A government rural school in Bolivia taught
by an American Mennonite teacher.

Grebel College is an inter-Mennonite institution affiliated with Waterloo University and located on its campus.

Northeastern Ohio (Wayne, Holmes, and Stark counties) is heavily populated by Mennonites. Ohio has more Old Order Amish than any other state. At least ten cheese factories are located in and around the small Swiss-like villages of Sugarcreek, Berlin, Charm, Farmerstown, Millersburg, and Walnut Creek. Many of the large Mennonite churches are made up of former Amish members who have affiliated with the Mennonites. The Mennonites in western Ohio, near Bluffton and Archbold, came to America over a hundred years later than the Pennsylvania Mennonites.

Northern Indiana has a strong Mennonite presence. Like the communities in Ontario, Ohio, and Pennsylvania it has many varieties of Amish and Mennonite people. Elkhart, Goshen, and the smaller towns of Middlebury, Shipshewanna, and Topeka are active centers of small industries, boat and house trailer factories. The countryside is dotted with one-room schools and neatly managed farms. On the south side of Goshen is Goshen College, a Mennonite four-year college, and Bethany Christian High School. The Associated Mennonite Biblical Seminaries and the Mennonite Board of Missions are located at Elkhart.

Central Kansas, the heart of the breadbasket of the nation, includes concentrations of both Swiss and Dutch Mennonite groups. Strongly represented are the General Conference Mennonites, the Mennonite Brethren, and the Church of God in Christ Mennonite. Many came from Poland and the Ukraine about 1873. With the aid of the Sante Fe Railroad, they acquired lands in Harvey and nearby counties. Bethel College in North Newton, Kansas, was founded by the General Conference Mennonites, Tabor College in Hillsboro by the Mennonite Brethren, and Hesston College in Hesston by the Pennsylvania Mennonites who had moved to Kansas. A large farm equipment factory, Hesston Manufacturing Company, was founded by Mennonite persons.

Another cluster of Mennonite groups is located in southeastern South Dakota, in Hutchinson and nearby counties. Several dialect-speaking groups are the Swiss who came by way of Poland and Russia, the Dutch-Prussian-Russian groups, and the Mennonites of Hutterite background. Much of the inter-Mennonite activity centers in the village of Freeman, the home of Freeman Junior College. *Schmeckfest,* "a festival of tasting," featuring foods from the various local ethnic groups, is celebrated there each year.

Southern Manitoba is Mennonite country. Winnipeg is the home of more Mennonites than any other city in the world. Originally these immigrants from South Russia settled in village-type clusters. In the meantime the Old Colony segment withdrew to Mexico. Today the small European-like villages of Blumenort, Reinland, and others, typify the early settlement patterns. There are several high schools and colleges in this area. The towns of Altona, Winkler, and Steinbach have large Mennonite populations.

In the far west, Mennonites are scattered throughout Saskatchewan and Alberta and from Alaska to Mexico. In southern British Columbia at least 40 Mennonite churches are located in or near Vancouver, Abbotsford, Yarrow, and Chilliwack and several inland towns. Mennonite families living in the Fraser Valley raise many fruits, vegetables, and berries. Western Oregon is the home of several thousand Mennonites. In California many Mennonites live in the central part of the state, in the San Joaquin Valley, in and around the towns of Fresno, Reedley, and Dinuba. Many of them are fruit and grape farmers. The Mennonite Brethren denomination operates Fresno Pacific College and a seminary.

There are numerous small Mennonite communities in the southern and central states. The Midwestern states, including Indiana, Illinois, and Iowa, have a number of farming communities. Sarasota, Florida, is the winter home of many Mennonite and Amish people.

A Mennonite-sponsored public auction where handmade quilts and crafts are sold.
Proceeds are used to support relief work.

Goshen College campus and library. A Mennonite affiliated institution
at Goshen, Indiana.

Social Networks

Vigorous social networks prevail on many levels among Mennonites. Part of this intimacy is due to the long-standing willingness to see themselves as being different from the prevailing culture. Part is the result of the compassionate and caring attitudes motivated by religious teachings—the willingness to be humble and to share rather than accumulate, possess, and protect. There are also many ethnic and kinship ties which put Mennonite people on the road. Their program of Christian worldwide relief service, voluntary service, and disaster service in American rural and urban regions, has sent their members in all directions. Families who wish to travel across America are aided by a hospitality network that permits them to stay in Mennonite homes and share common interests.

The Mennonite World Conference which meets every six years is a multicultural network drawing people from every part of the world. Its purpose is fellowship, inspiration, learning, and stimulation rather than policy formation. This diverse gathering brings Mennonites together from the country and the city, from the poor and the wealthy, from the educated and the uneducated, from liberal and conservative orientations, and from democratic and dictatorial nations. This gathering stimulates world consciousness, and in spite of the widely different traditions the various Mennonite subgroups find among themselves, the participants also discover the ties which they hold in common.

These ties include a deep commitment to the Anabaptist tradition of discipleship, living peaceful lives, expressing love in service, and calling into question unjust structures that conflict with the teaching of Jesus. Their mission in the world is to form clusters and communities of believers who live together in harmony, and who find hope in the spiritual quality of their relationships.

Sense of Mission

The Mennonite understanding of mission involves far more than the individual's relationship to God. The practice of brotherhood and Christian love in human relationships is essential to the redemptive process. Love, for them, is not a mere sentiment or emotion, but a stable biblical way of life. The enduring qualities of gentleness, humility, and consistent peace witness have attracted individuals from other backgrounds to the Mennonite brotherhood. The several hundred Mennonite missionaries serving in various parts of the globe not only teach conversion and personal commitment to the faith, but they stimulate the development of caring communities.

Church membership is restricted to those who share the principles and accept the discipline of the church. Members cannot plead personal belief in God as a substitute for proper Christian conduct. They fellowship in small groups, and they admonish and help each other.

Their caring communities find many ways to support needy persons in unpretentious ways. Mennonites, like the Society of Friends and Church of the Brethren, frequently testify to the government against conscription for military training in the nation's capital. Some denounce excessive profits in wartime, and refuse to buy toy guns, tanks, and bombers for their children.

Mennonite agencies help young people find relevant work and service assignments in needy places in the world. As conscientious objectors during wartime many young people served in mental hospitals, public health and sanitation projects, conservation programs, and human guinea pig experiments. In some instances their services led to institutional reform and better patient care. Today hundreds of Mennonite young people continue to serve for one or two years in a program of Voluntary Service without salary. The beneficiaries of their services include migrant camps, mental hospitals, training schools for delinquent children, and community health and welfare services.

Mennonite communities across North America have organized a

Mennonite Disaster Service volunteer workers.

formal coast-to-coast network called Mennonite Disaster Service (MDS). When floods, tornadoes, or other forms of emergency strike, volunteers come to the aid of stricken people regardless of creed or race by cleaning, building, and restoring homes. MDS is registered with the National Red Cross.

Mennonite persons engaged in business and in the professions have developed a new awareness of social and economic injustices. To develop a Christian social conscience they meet regularly to promote Christian social ethics. Modern Mennonites have entered virtually all occupations, from accounting to well drilling. Like the Mennonite-Quakers of Colonial Pennsylvania who were among the first to protest slavery, they have retained a tender conscience and a sense of mission.

Leadership and Education

Attitudes toward education among the Mennonites vary with the type of community life practiced by each of the groups (whether open or closed to modernization). Among the plain Mennonite groups, formal education beyond the elementary grades is not only considered unnecessary but harmful to their community life. Their children, like the Amish, attend church-operated country schools, staffed by their own members. The "fancy" or modernized Mennonites operate high schools and colleges. Some are faculty members in major universities. There is a certain amount of tension between "educated" and "uneducated" Mennonites. For example, the Old Order groups feel that those parents who send their children to schools of higher education risk losing their humility and possibly their faith. The more formally educated Mennonites tend to feel that the plain groups run the risk of becoming socially stagnant. On the whole, however, the various Mennonite groups tend to respect each other's difference as they promote the gospel of reconciliation and peace.

Throughout Mennonite history literacy has been emphasized, since

Mennonite students of sign language perform a "show of hands."

reading the Bible is important to a knowledge of salvation. The Old Order groups stress training for life, instruction in the basics such as reading, writing, and arithmetic, and the moral teachings of the Bible. They carefully avoid the "pagan" enlightenment of higher education, the philosophical and intellectual studies which they feel lead to self-exaltation, pride, enjoyment of power, and the arts of war and violence. Their goals are humility, simple living, and resignation to the will of God, and these are achieved by recitation, memorization, and trusting relationships between teacher and pupil. An outstanding teacher among Mennonites in colonial times was Christopher Dock who wrote a textbook on methods of teaching. He emphasized character development, and in addition to teaching the basic skills, he also taught art. Many of his beautiful illuminated manuscripts or *Fraktur-Schriften* are preserved in historical libraries.

The plain or Old Order Mennonites wish to maintain their rural farming communities, and their country schools help them to acquire the appropriate skills and attitudes. The training acquired in these schools aids them to achieve their religious ideals, a limited separation from the world, useful manual skills, and the maintenance of a disciplined and orderly life close to the soil. These schools are taught, not by college-trained teachers, but by their own members who acquire the needed skills by a system of apprenticeship. The church-community selects teachers who are qualified by example. The plain Mennonites are not alone in maintaining church schools, for several of the large Mennonite groups also operate Christian elementary schools and high schools.

The method of choosing leaders or pastors differs widely among Mennonite bodies. Among the most modernized groups, a single trained pastor is chosen by the church in a professional manner and paid a salary. Among the plain groups, leaders without formal training are chosen from among the membership in the local congregation. The church is run "from the bottom up," with members maintaining active participation and strong consensus in respect to policy making. The chosen leader is "servant of all." Some of the plain groups select their leaders by nomination, followed by the casting of the lot. In the best Mennonite tradition, leaders see themselves as servants rather than a special class of clergy set above or apart from the lay members.

Backstage

The Mennonites, like other subcultures, must cope with the ills, mistakes, and recurring human problems of their own making. These recurring afflictions, often shielded from the public view, have been termed the backstage of a culture. Mennonites are not free from mental illness, from gaps between belief and practice, and from individual, family, or community tragedies.

Since Mennonites strive to live out their faith and to achieve consistency in brotherhood, social harmony, and humility, the most recurring afflictions tend to be the opposite of these qualities. Thus the trend toward mistrust, factionalism, jealousies, and feuding are ugly realities with which they have to cope. These afflictions surface when members assume a judgmental posture, when they are quick to suspect the motives of others, and when they pass on gossip, especially of those who are envied or who are competitiors in striving for humility. Mennonite history is fraught with many divisions. Nevertheless, the large diversity of practice expressed in groups within the broader Mennonite world allows many individuals to identify with the faith who would otherwise reject it.

By conventional American standards, some Mennonites are wealthy. They are not always the most "worldly" ones. Some accept the conventional standards of affluence, de-emphasize their differences, and seek greater social acceptance by their neighbors.

Tensions within and between Mennonite groups in North America persist, and in the search for an authentic living faith, they are normal. Those who feel threatened by the loss of their cherished customs, their childhood associations, intimacy, and family life, use the church to

Crafts made by South American Indians are sold through the Self-Help program of
the Mennonite Central Committee.

oppose change. Others try to use the church as an instrument of renewal by proclaiming to all cultures the gospel of love and reconciliation. Some hold that individual conversion is all that matters, while others are sensitive to social injustices and try to help the disadvantaged and the oppressed. In the face of nuclear destruction and a high percentage of taxes going for defense, some are advocating nonpayment of war taxes. Others consider such actions unchristian. Another segment is unhappy with the bureaucratic, sterile character of the large churches and feels that a new movement of house-churches should be formed. In the absence of a platform for healthy discourse these tensions frequently become divisive.

On a deeper level, a dialogue prevails between those who follow an articulate verbal orientation and the "old order" who are committed to silent discourse. The latter will refrain from argument. Modern, educated Mennonites tend to emphasize rationality, individuality, enlightenment, and scholarly studies. Such tendencies move them closer to the structures of the world and away from the maintenance of a closed community. Those committed to a strong tradition take their cues from collective awareness and from the symbols of unity and community. They will not speculate about words of Scripture over which the more educated may argue. For them, ultimate values do not exist in scholarly texts, creeds, or in a centralized authority, but in the example of Christ himself.

The Mennonites are an influential minority. They are an example, a witness against war and the injustices of the larger society. They call into question some of the extremes within Christendom itself. Their inability to achieve their high ideals keeps them humble. Should they ever become a majority they might lose their effectiveness, their gentleness, and their compassion.

Mennonite and Related Denominations in North America*

———

Mennonite Church
General Conference Mennonite Church
Mennonite Brethren Church
Old Order Amish
Brethren in Christ
Old Order Mennonite
Hutterian Brethren
Church of God in Christ, Mennonite (Holdeman)
Beachy Amish Mennonite
Old Colony Mennonite
Evangelical Mennonite Conference, Canada
Evangelical Mennonite Brethren
Evangelical Mennonite Church
Sommerfelder Mennonite Church
Evangelical Mennonite Mission Conference
Chortitzer Mennonite Conference
Rhinelander Mennonite Church
Old Order River Brethren
Reformed Mennonites

Mennonite Colleges and Seminaries

———

Associated Mennonite Biblical Seminaries, Elkhart, Indiana
Bethel College, North Newton, Kansas
Bluffton College, Bluffton, Ohio
Canadian Mennonite Bible College, Winnipeg
Conrad Grebel College, Waterloo, Ontario
Eastern Mennonite College and Seminary, Harrisonburg, Virginia
Freeman College, Freeman, South Dakota
Fresno Pacific College, Fresno, California
Goshen College, Goshen, Indiana
Hesston College, Hesston, Kansas
Mennonite Brethren Bible College, Winnipeg
Mennonite Brethren Biblical Seminary, Fresno, California
Rosedale Bible Institute, Irwin, Ohio
Tabor College, Hillsboro, Kansas

*Arranged from most to least membership.

Selected References

HISTORY AND BELIEFS

Introduction to Mennonite History, C. J. Dyck, ed. Scottdale, Pa.: Herald Press, 1981.

Anabaptism: Neither Catholic Nor Protestant, Walter Klaassen. Waterloo, Ont.: Conrad Press, 1971.

In the Fullness of Time: 150 Years of Mennonite Sojourn in Russia, by Walter Quiring and Helen Bartel. Waterloo, Ont.: 1974. A pictorial history.

The Politics of Jesus, John H. Yoder. Grand Rapids, Mich.: Eerdmans, 1972. A creative study of the social and ethical teachings of Jesus with implications for modern believers.

INFORMATION AND REFERENCE WORKS

Mennonite Information Center, 2209 Millstream Road, Lancaster, Pa. 17602. This regional center for travelers has a display of Mennonite activities and publications, and responds to inquiries by mail or telephone (717) 299–0954.

Mennonite Encyclopedia. Four volumes. Available in most large libraries. Mennonite Publishing House, Scottdale, Pa.

Mennonite Weekly Review. An inter-Mennonite newspaper. Herald Publishing Co., 129 West 6th Street, Newton Kansas.

CULTURE AND PRACTICE

Woman Liberated, Lois G. Clemens. Scottdale, Pa.: Herald Press. Discusses the role of women in the Mennonite community.

Day of Disaster, Katie Funk Wiebe. Scottdale, Pa.: Herald Press. Description of Mennonite Disaster Service activity.

Mennonite Community Cookbook, Mary Emma Showalter. Scottdale, Pa.: Herald Press. Traditional Mennonite recipes.

More-with-Less Cookbook, Doris Janzen Longacre. Scottdale, Pa.: Herald Press, 1976. Third world recipes chosen for their simplicity and good nutrition.

Living More with Less. Doris Janzen Longacre. Scottdale, Pa.: Herald Press, 1980. Suggestions and models for simple ways of living.

FICTION

Pilgrim Aflame, Myron Augsburger. Scottdale, Pa.: Herald Press. Story of a Mennonite leader who faced martyrdom.

The Blue Mountains of China, Rudy Wiebe. Toronto: McClelland and Stewart. A novel based on Mennonite life in Russia and Asia.

Skippack School, Marguerite de Angeli. Doubleday. For Children.

Days of Terror, Barbara Smucker. Scottdale, Pa.: Herald Press. Juvenile. Describes revolution and mass exit from Russia to Canada.

47

FILM

"606" The Persistence of Community. Documentary film, 28 min. color. Mennonites in Shenandoah Valley of Virginia. Distributed by Buller Films, Inc., 1053 Main St., Henderson, Neb. 68371.

The Mennonites of Ontario. Documentary film, 30 minutes. Available from Buller Films, Inc. (see above), or from The Meetinghouse, St. Jacobs, Ontario.

CREDITS: PHOTOGRAPHS AND ILLUSTRATIONS
Mark Beach 32 bottom, 35; Arthur Driedger 27 top; Gerhard Ens 27 bottom; Jan Gleysteen 10, 15 top and bottom; Goshen College 36; Heinz Hindorf 24; Amos Hoover 16 top right; John A. Hostetler 16 top left; David L. Hunsberger 12; Claude Jerome 23 top; James King, cover, 9, 20, 29; Muriel Kirkpatrick, 2 map; Jan Luyken 5; Alain Masson 7; Mennonite Central Committee 32 top, 39, 44; Marie Moyer 31; John Ruth 10, 23 bottom; Fred Wilson 19; John C. Yoder 41.

THE AUTHOR: John A. Hostetler is Professor of Anthropology and Sociology, Temple University, Philadelphia, Pennsylvania.